Downsized UP

Downsized UP

Trusting God Through Your Layoff

Lillie J. Cameron

A Division of WINEPRESS PUBLISHING

Printed in the United States of America

Packaged by Pleasant Word, a Division of WinePress Publishing, PO Box 428, Enumclaw, WA 98022. The views expressed or implied in this work do not necessarily reflect those of WinePress Publishing. The author(s) is ultimately responsible for the design, content, and editorial accuracy of this work.

Unless otherwise noted, Scripture quotations in this book are taken from the King James Version of the Bible.

ISBN 1-57921-529-7
Library of Congress Catalog Card Number: 2002115813

With gratitude to my Lord and Savior

"Blessed is she who has believed that what the Lord
has said to her will be accomplished!"

Luke 1:45 NIV

Contents

Section I: Let Go

Section II: Lean Hard to Stand Firm

Section III: Stop and Ask for Directions

Section IV: Change

Section V: Green Pastures in the Desert

Section VI: Seeds and Harvest

Section VII: Networking

Section VIII: Next!

Epilogue

To my mother, Elizabeth Love

Who has always been an example of strength
and courage because of her unshakable faith.

Dedicated to other Women of Great Faith

Evangelist Katie B. Powell

Evangelist Lillian Ricks

Reverend Esther James Mitchell
Reverend Lucille Lewis Jackson
J.W. James Memorial African Methodist
Episcopal Church

and to

Sakeena Davis who has flown to her reward

Acknowledgments

To my son, Duane Cameron, for pushing me to write. In his own distinctive way it was a mixture of support and harassment, but I appreciate it. Thanks for being my role model as you daily exhibit the passion for your God given gifts and talents.

To Kevin Cabell who said, "Just write; whatever you write will be good." Thanks for always being there and believing in me.

To my sisterhood—my close friends and the Sunday school class at J.W. James Memorial A.M.E. Church. You all know who you are. Thanks for listening, chastising and uplifting me when I need it.

To the Saturday morning writers group, thanks for your insight and encouragement as we all strive to tell our stories.

Special love to my siblings Linda, Stanley, and Renita, and my nieces and nephews. Thanks for always allowing me to be myself. I pray for joy on your journey to fulfilling God's purpose for your lives.

Foreword

Though I have never doubted that my friend Carolyn would one day publish her first book, it was a surprise and honor that she asked me to write the foreword.

Carolyn and I initially met ten years ago as employees serving in the same diversity network. Our friendship blossomed along with five other employees who participated in a company-sponsored training class. Following that course, we bonded and attended plays, football games, housewarmings, birthday and graduation celebrations with our families.

Though I considered our friendship a strong one, it was taken to another level when I accepted Jesus Christ as my Lord and Savior in 1998. I already considered Carolyn a sister, but now she was a sister in Christ. There is a way of communicating with a fellow born-again believer that may seem a little rough to a non believer who doesn't understand that "For whom the Lord loveth, he chasteneth" (Hebrews 12:6a). When one of us would call the other about a challenging situation, neither of us would hesitate to go to the Word of God and remind the other what sayeth the Lord.

Carolyn's faith always amazed me. It has provided insight and direction for me since the layoff in early 2001. Even though every fiber in my being wanted to leave due to some difficult circumstances, I was terrified of being unemployed. Ironically, I had just heard a sermon the previous Sunday entitled, "It's Time to Leave." Who did I call when I arrived home? Carolyn. She said, "Have peace. It's a sign of answered prayer."

I have been very distraught at times with the competitive job market over the past year but Carolyn and I have worked through this together, constantly standing on God's word. In Matthew 6, Jesus asks us why we worry about what we will eat, drink or wear. God has provided manna every day since I have left. He has never forsaken me. When I tend to worry, I call Carolyn, and her faith calms and amazes me more now than ever. She reminds me that what God has for us will come when He is ready and when we are ready to receive it. That has been a challenge for me since I want so much to take control. God will move when He gets the glory.

I thank God for His promises and the blessing of Carolyn as my friend. May her words bless you as they have me.

Janice Brewer

Psalm 86:6–7 NIV
"Hear my prayer, O Lord; listen to my cry for mercy. In the day of my trouble I will call to you, for you will answer me."

Hebrews 4:16 NIV
"Let us then approach the throne of grace with confidence, so that we may receive mercy and find grace to help us in our time of need."

1 Thessalonians 4:16–18 NIV
"Be joyful always; pray continually; give thanks in all circumstances, for this is God's will for you in Christ Jesus."

Introduction

I had just returned from spring-break vacation right before I was laid off after working thirteen years at a Fortune 500 company. I didn't panic or feel sad when I got the news. I honestly don't know what my reaction would have been if it had not been for my relaxed state of mind.

As I packed my personal items after the exit session, I still didn't feel emotional even though it was with a sense of finality. It was undeniably an end to a great deal of professional and personal milestones shared with the same familiar faces over the years. What crossed my mind were some short term benefits for being let go:

- I didn't have to read the thirty-seven emails in my inbox.
- I didn't have to respond to any urgent voicemails.
- I didn't have to attend any meetings or stress out because of endless deadlines.

The best part was no commute the next morning.

I had to snicker at how many times I thought about my "to do" list while I was on vacation. In the end I left everything without a second glance and without guilt because I had given my best. As I drove out of the parking lot, I was at peace. It wasn't a deep spiritual revelation but I knew God was going to take care of me. The layoff was out of my control. Finally the tears came. I cried and said out loud, "God I don't know what You're doing, but could I please have the summer off?"

Months later, I still have a tranquil spirit. In between my job search I focused on things that were important to me, quality time with family and friends and what I desired in my next career move. I also had the opportunity to pursue a dream that had been shoved behind too many other priorities over the years. The downsizing experience has provided time and freedom to develop my voice as a writer.

This book is not an in-depth guide with the best tips for resume writing, interviewing, networking, and enhancing your job skills to land your next position. Hopefully, as you read, you will understand that layoffs cannot take you under when you trust God and allow Him to guide you as you search and wait in faith.

God has been in control throughout my season of unemployment. He has proven over and over his divine insight, timing and sense of humor. The more I rely on God the more I feel "downsized up."

LET GO

Psalm 121:1–2 KJV
"I will lift up mine eyes unto the hills, from whence cometh my help? My help cometh from the Lord, which made heaven and earth."

1 Peter 5:7 KJV
"Casting all your care upon him; for he careth for you."

Jeremiah 29:11–12 NIV
"For I know the plans I have for you," declares the Lord, "plans to prosper you and not to harm you, plans to give you hope and a future. Then you will call upon me and come and pray to me, and I will listen to you."

Chapter 1

We Have to Let You . . .

I t happened. You can now identify with the "poor" strangers you have been hearing about in the news. You have been laid off, too. Whether you had an idea it was coming or if you were totally surprised, it's something to reckon with. Your first reaction may have been, "Why me?" You worked hard, stayed late, came in when you were ill, and this is what you get. Worse case scenario is after stripping your employee ID, you were immediately escorted out of the door like a criminal. In shock? That's understandable. Angry? Not a surprise.

Traumatic? Yes, but if God still wanted you there you would still be there regardless of the company's bottom line. Why you? Why not you? If it can happen to others it can happen to you. There are some emotional and financial adjustments to be made, but you are still in one piece. You will get through this. Face it, come to grips and pray for direction.

God is waiting to hear from you and He won't let you go.

You are no longer working, but God is. He is still working on your behalf. Don't lay Him off!

After your hasty exit, what can God work out for you?

_____

_____

_____

_____

_____

_____

_____

_____

_____

_____

_____

_____

_____

_____

_____

_____

_____

_____

_____

_____

Job 5:6–9 NIV
"For hardship does not spring from the soil, nor does
trouble sprout from the ground. Yet man is born to
trouble as surely as sparks fly upward. But if it were I, I
would appeal to God; I would lay my cause before him.
He performs wonders that cannot be fathomed, miracles
that cannot be counted."

Hebrews 13:5–6 NIV
"Keep your lives free from the love of money and be
content with what you have, because God has said, 'Never
will I leave you; never will I forsake you.'"

"So we say with confidence, 'The Lord is my helper; I
will not be afraid, what can man do to me?'"

Job 22:21–22 NIV
"Submit to God and be at peace with him; in this way
prosperity will come to you. Accept instruction from his
mouth and lay up his words in your heart."

Chapter 2

· ·

You Lost Your Job,
Not Your Status

God does not operate by any silver-spoon principles. He never valued the real you because of the level of your position, so it's irrelevant to Him whether you pushed the broom or purchased the brooms.

You may be vulnerable right now and even believe you've lost your identity with the loss of your job. It probably doesn't help when others tell you, "Things could be a lot worse." That's true, but the layoff tops your list of bad things at the moment.

Consider this: What if you experienced a number of catastrophic losses one right after the other? There is a narrative in the Bible about a rich man who enjoyed a large family and owned lots of servants, land, and animals. Within a short span, his sons and daughters lost their lives at the same time, his servants were killed, and his animals either died or were stolen. On top of this, the man's body was ravaged with disease, and he was in constant physical pain while trying to cope with his grief.

This is the story of Job. He lost everything, but never cursed God during his suffering, because he was grateful for all of his past blessings. He also knew whatever he was going through was God's will. The Lord honored Job's faith and brought him through the trial. He also blessed Job to become a father again and restored more land and animals than he had before.

What confirms your importance in life? Is it the job that you had, or your faith in God to restore everything just like He did for Job.

Isaiah 55:9–11 NIV
"As the heavens are higher than the earth, so are my ways higher than your ways and my thoughts than your thoughts. As the rain and the snow come down from heaven, and do not return to it without watering the earth and making it bud and flourish, so that it yields seed for the sower and bread for the eater, so is my word that goes out from my mouth: It will not return to me empty, but will accomplish what I desire and achieve the purpose for which I sent it."

Nehemiah 9:19–20 NIV
"Because of your great compassion you did not abandon them in the desert. By day the pillar of cloud did not cease to guide them on their path, nor the pillar of fire by night to shine on the way they were to take. You gave your good Spirit to instruct them. You did not withhold your manna from their mouths, and you gave them water for their thirst."

Psalm 37:4–6 NIV
"Delight yourself in the Lord and he will give you the desires of your heart. Commit your way to the Lord; trust in him and he will do this: He will make your righteousness shine like the dawn, the justice of your cause like the noonday sun."

Chapter 3

Don't Stand Still
in the Heat

There's a saying that you should "bloom where you are planted." You can't control the elements, and you certainly have no input on your company's downsizing but you can bloom in this "drought" experience like cactus thrives in the desert.

If you stand still and harp on the fact that you are unemployed, the heat of the circumstances will beat you down. Try standing in faith. You will move forward knowing that God will send another job just as He sent you the last one.

God is trustworthy and He *does* control the elements.

How are you? How do you really feel about the layoff?

_____

_____

_____

_____

_____

_____

_____

_____

_____

_____

_____

_____

_____

_____

_____

_____

_____

_____

_____

LEAN HARD TO STAND FIRM

Psalm 16:7–8 NIV
"I will praise the Lord, who counsels me; even at night my heart instructs me. I have set the Lord always before me. Because he is at my right hand, I will not be shaken."

Psalm 121:3–4 KJV
"He will not suffer thy foot to be moved; he who keepeth thee will not slumber. Behold, he who keepeth Israel shall neither slumber nor sleep."

Nahum 1:7 KJV
"The Lord is good, a stronghold in the day of trouble, and he knoweth those who trust in him."

Chapter 4

God Was Not Sleeping On The Job

Whether you were surprised or not when you got the news, God was not up in Heaven playing out any of these scenarios:

- OOPS! Sorry, I didn't see this coming.
- It was out of My control.
- I have no idea what you are going to do.

God expects us to ask for help because we can expect Him to take action. It's an insult to consider Him a fair-weather friend. If you relied on Him when you had a job, you must definitely trust him now that you are unemployed.

Look up with confidence, God did not delegate His responsibility in your time of need.

God is never confused about what you need at any given time. He will also never take away what you truly need without replacing that void.

_____

_____

_____

_____

_____

_____

_____

_____

_____

_____

_____

_____

_____

_____

_____

_____

_____

_____

Psalm 131:1–2 NIV
"My heart is not proud, O Lord, my eyes are not haughty;
I do not concern myself with great matters or things too
wonderful for me. But I have stilled and quieted my soul;
like a weaned child with its mother, like a weaned child
is my soul within me."

Lamentations 3:57 KJV
"Thou drewest near in the day that I called upon thee;
thou saidst, Fear not."

Matthew 11:28–30 NIV
"Come to me, all you who are weary and burdened, and
I will give you rest. Take my yoke upon you and learn
from me, for I am gentle and humble in heart, and you
will find rest for your souls. For my yoke is easy and my
burden is light."

Chapter 5

. . . .

It's Okay to Rest
By the Still Waters

Don't feel guilty about still loving yourself or nurturing your self esteem. The layoff was business, not personal. While you are watching your budget, don't stop living. Routine can be comforting during this major change. In between the job hunt, do the things you have always wanted to do, but didn't have the time.

1) Spend more time with God through prayer and meditation.
2) Take classes to develop new skills
3) Start/finish long overdue home or personal projects.
4) Take your dream vacation if you can afford it.
5) Volunteer at your church or in the community.
6) Go to the entertainment venues during the day and avoid the weekend crowds.

On a lighter note, once in awhile sleep in late, linger over coffee at your own kitchen table or catch up on your reading.

Be kind to yourself. God is not punishing you. This is just an unexpected break; when it's over God will let you know.

Philippians 4:4–7 NIV
"Rejoice in the Lord always. I will say it again: Rejoice! Let your gentleness be evident to all. The Lord is near. Do not be anxious about anything, but in everything, by prayer and petition, with thanksgiving, present your requests to God. And the peace of God, which transcends all understanding, will guard your hearts and your minds in Christ Jesus."

2nd Corinthians 4:17–18 NIV
"For our light and momentary troubles are achieving for us an eternal glory that far outweighs them all. So we fix our eyes not on what is seen, but on what is unseen. For what is seen is temporary, but what is unseen is eternal."

1 Peter 5:10 NIV
"And the God of all grace, who called you to his eternal glory in Christ after you have suffered a little while, will himself restore you and make you strong, firm and steadfast."

Chapter 6
Don't Count Me Out

Family and friends will take your cue on how they view the layoff. When you take your eyes off the circumstances and look at God, they can see your peace and realize this is not going to take you under. Your optimistic attitude will help them accept it better.

They don't want to see you depressed, but they may not understand why you can still smile and have a good time. Your faith may appear to be a façade, and it may irritate your associates who are also unemployed. Guard yourself in the safety zone; you are walking in the "Peace that passes understanding." Just tell your inner circle you are trusting God and waiting on Him for the next move.

As long as you can trust the One Who is controlling your situation, you can still be yourself. When everyone sees that you are okay, they can support you with the same positive energy you project.

God is the only one important enough to look down on you. He does it to watch over you.

Matthew 23:12 NIV
"For whoever exalts himself will be humbled, and whoever humbles himself will be exalted. "

Jeremiah 17:5–8 NIV
"This is what the Lord says: 'Cursed is the one who trusts
in man, who depends on flesh for his strength and whose
heart turns away from the Lord. He will be like a bush in
the wastelands; he will not see prosperity when it comes.
He will dwell in the parched places of the desert, in a
salt land where no one lives. But blessed is the man who
trusts in the Lord, whose confidence is in him. He will
be like a tree planted by the water that sends out its roots
by the stream. It does not fear when heat comes; its leaves
are always green. It has no worries in a year of drought
and never fails to bear fruit.'"

Psalm 37:23–24 NIV
"If the Lord delights in a man's way, he makes his steps
firm; though he stumble, he will not fall, for the Lord
upholds him with his hand."

Psalm 62:5–8 KJV
"My soul, wait thou only upon God; for my expectation
is from him. He only is my rock and my salvation; he is
my defense; I shall not be moved. In God is my salvation
and my glory, the rock of my strength; my refuge is in
God. Trust in him at all times, ye people; pour out your
heart before him. God is a refuge for us."

Chapter 7

Let the Real Manager Take Over

Have you ever looked in the Bible and a verse jumps out that seems to have been written just for you and whatever is going on in your life at the time? It's reassurance that God not only manages heaven and earth, He's also thinking about you, too. When God drops a scripture into your spirit, it becomes your special connection with Him. His Word is filled with love and encouragement, and it is His desire to comfort us in all circumstances.

The text that spoke directly to me was Jeremiah 17:5–8. I read it every morning to set the tone for my day. It's a promise of abundant provision during the tough times.

There's a scripture with your name on it. Claim it for daily confirmation that God is in control of everything that revolves around you.

STOP AND ASK FOR DIRECTIONS

Isaiah 30:21 NIV
"Whether you turn to the right or to the left, your ears will hear a voice behind you, saying, 'This is the way; walk in it.'"

Psalm 91:1–2 NIV
"He who dwells in the shelter of the Most High will rest in the shadow of the Almighty. I will say of the Lord, 'He is my refuge and my fortress, my God, in whom I trust.'"

Proverbs 16:9 NIV
"In his heart a man plans his course, but the Lord determines his steps."

Chapter 8

* *

Right This Way

Usually without question we will follow the directions of an "official usher" when we are guests in a public place. We expect them to tell us when to enter, where to sit, hand us a program, and give easy directions to the closest restroom. We assume they know everything there is to know to make our visit comfortable. Funny, we don't necessarily give God as much credibility as an usher, even though He can see where we need to go and will kindly direct us when we choose to follow.

Years ago I was whining and crying all the time because of a very stressful job. One afternoon when I had all that I thought I could take, I called out to God. He directed me to go to a familiar pond that was near my workplace. Fortunately it was lunchtime and I left right away. As I sat restlessly on the bench, I noticed some ducks swimming toward me. The ducks were in a V formation following the leader closely. My mind started rambling with other thoughts as I waited for something to happen. When I looked up again, I noticed that the ducks had reached the other side of the pond. They were quacking and flapping their wings joyfully.

After several minutes the leader started to swim away. The other ducks also fell in line. As they swam toward my end of the pond, I watched transfixed. The leader's head was straight and tall. I realized the ducks were following in complete trust.

They didn't know whether the water was going to be too shallow or too deep. They simply followed the leader.

If we allow God to lead us through this layoff, there is no need to figure out when the trials will be too shallow or too deep. We can trust Him to help us cross to the other side.

Romans 8:35, 37 NIV
"Who shall separate us from the love of Christ? Shall trouble or hardship or persecution or famine or nakedness or danger or sword? . . . No, in all these things we are more than conquerors through him who loved us."

Psalm 5:12 NIV
"For surely, O Lord, you bless the righteous; you surround them with your favor as with a shield."

1 Chronicles 16:11 NIV
"Look to the Lord and his strength; seek his face always."

Chapter 9
Red Light, Green Light

Sometimes God will nudge us and ask, "Can I drive?" He gives us free will and sometimes we shy away from allowing Him to steer our lives through a crisis. It's been said that "God cannot steer a parked car," so we confine our greatest resource to the back seat.

Think about it. If you are angry at God about this whole layoff business you've shut Him out of the restoration. If He can drive the process you will avoid a lot of headaches in your job search. With a little faith, He will take over the wheel. Only God knows the traffic jams and construction zones up ahead. He even has His own rules of the road.

Yellow Light:
A transition is coming. God is ready to make a change in our lives.

Red Light:
Stop. Be still. Rest on His promises.

Green Light:
Everything is in divine order. Proceed with confidence and gratitude.

The next time the Lord asks you to let Him drive, move over to the passenger's side and settle in for a peaceful ride. Whether God takes you on His expressway or the long scenic route, don't tell Him how to get where you are going, especially when you don't have a clue about your next destination. God does, and He always starts out with the right directions.

So move over, no need to get lost on this trip.

CHANGE

Psalm 139:15–16 NIV
"My frame was not hidden from you when I was made in the secret place. When I was woven together in the depths of the earth, your eyes saw my unformed body. All the days ordained for me were written in your book before one of them came to be."

Isaiah 50:7 KJV
"For the Lord God will help me; therefore shall I not be confounded; therefore have I set my face like a flint, and I know that I shall not be ashamed."

James 1:5–8 NIV
"If any of you lacks wisdom, he should ask God, who gives generously to all without finding fault, and it will be given to him. But when he asks, he must believe and not doubt, because he who doubts is like a wave of the sea, blown and tossed by the wind. That man should not think he will receive anything from the Lord; he is a double-minded man, unstable in all he does."

Chapter 10

Actors Do It All the Time

Actors change their personalities and appearance for their current roles. They must take cues from the director to do whatever is necessary to make their character come alive.

You have a new starring role without auditioning for the part. Your switch from employee to job seeker happened overnight. You can either act on basic instinct or shine with insight from the director who casts all your roles.

If you follow God's script, you can still have joy, though you may be stretched and challenged. It doesn't matter whether you are doing a cameo or an extended run, the job-seeker role will take your faith to a new level. Remember, God is a master at productions. He not only directs, He writes and edits too. He always has final approval on how your story ends.

Hoping for an encore? Or are you ready for new scenery?

_____

_____

_____

_____

_____

_____

_____

_____

_____

_____

_____

_____

_____

_____

_____

_____

_____

_____

_____

Lamentations 3:22–24 NIV
"Because of the Lord's great love we are not consumed, for his compassions never fail. They are new every morning; great is your faithfulness. I say to myself, 'The Lord is my portion; therefore I will wait for him.'"

Galatians 6:9 KJV
"And let us not be weary in well doing; for in due season we shall reap, if we faint not."

Hebrews 10:35–36 NIV
"So do not throw away your confidence; it will be richly rewarded. You need to persevere so that when you have done the will of God, you will receive what he has promised."

Chapter 11

· ·

Color Shift

Leaves are seasonal. They usher in a renewal of life in the spring, the summer leaf provides shade from the heat, and autumn leaves are a cornucopia of beautiful reds, gold, and wine before they die and fall to the ground.

Whether you were an individual contributor or part of a team at your former job, you were a unique color because of your particular way of doing things. Your season there is over, but unlike the leaves, you won't be raked up and discarded. You will bring the same skills and expertise to your new position with even more self confidence.

The layoff can season your character. It's a color shift.

1 Thessalonians 5:24 KJV
"Faithful is he that calleth you, who also will do it."

1 Corinthians 2:9 NIV
"No eye has seen, no ear has heard, no mind has conceived what God has prepared for those who love him."

Psalm 34:4–5 NIV
"I sought the Lord, and he answered me; he delivered me from all my fears. Those who look to him are radiant; their faces are never covered with shame."

Chapter 12

Pink and Gold Is Not a Bad Combination

What's better, a false sense of security on a boring job or looking with anticipation for something more suitable? If we are honest, some of us continue in jobs that no longer motivate us to get up in the morning. We are there because we have families to take care of and bills to pay. When you are tapped on the shoulder to leave during a downsizing, your false sense of security changes in an instant.

You may be surprised about what you feel deep down. I was. I wasn't angry or bitter about my layoff, and I never felt a sense of loss. If you feel the same, don't be ashamed.

The pink slip made it possible to do what you wouldn't on your own—leave without appearing irresponsible. Suddenly the headaches and resentment you associated with the job are gone.

God knew you could handle a layoff at this particular time. He can help you conquer your worst enemy right now—your own fear. Let God use that pink slip as a gold passport to a journey He has mapped out just for you.

What's your passion? Can your part-time hobby yield full-time revenue?

Is finding your passion after the pink slip a blessing in disguise?

_____

_____

_____

_____

_____

_____

_____

_____

_____

_____

_____

_____

_____

_____

_____

_____

_____

_____

Proverbs 19:20–21 NIV
"Listen to advice and accept instruction, and in the end
you will be wise. Many are the plans in a man's heart,
but it is the Lord's purpose that prevails."

Hebrews 12:10–11 NIV
"Our fathers disciplined us for a little while as they
thought best; but God disciplines us for our good, that
we may share in his holiness. No discipline seems pleasant at the time, but painful. Later on, however, it pro-
duces a harvest of righteousness and peace for those who
have been trained by it."

Isaiah 26:12 NIV
"Lord, you establish peace for us; all that we have accomplished you have done for us."

Chapter 13

. . . But God

Every time you see "But God" in the Bible, it signals a heads-up that He is about to cause someone or some situation to change according to His plan. It's often the transition required to sweep away the old to make room for the new.

How many blessings have swept by us because we held on too long or continued to look back when God was trying to close a door in our lives? What does that have to do with a layoff? Here are some blessings I received despite it.

-Yes, I was laid off, but God flooded me with peace.

-Yes, my steady source of income ceased, but God never allowed my bank account to empty.

-Yes, I didn't know what my next job would be, but God had already decided my next assignment before the layoff.

What seemed like a painful transition gave me the discipline to see a different level.

You preferred to stay, but God has other plans. What steps can you take to move out of your comfort zone?

_____

_____

_____

_____

_____

_____

_____

_____

_____

_____

_____

_____

_____

_____

_____

_____

_____

_____

_____

_____

GREEN PASTURES IN THE DESERT

Psalm 23 NIV
"The Lord is my shepherd, I shall not be in want.
He makes me lie down in green pastures,
he leads me beside quiet waters,
he restores my soul.
He guides me in paths of righteousness for his name's
sake.
Even though I walk
through the valley of the shadow of death,
I will fear no evil,
for you are with me;
your rod and your staff,
they comfort me.
You prepare a table before me
in the presence of my enemies.
You anoint my head with oil;
my cup overflows.
Surely goodness and love will follow me
all the days of my life
and I will dwell in the house of the Lord
forever."

Psalm 145:15–16 KJV
"The eyes of all wait upon thee; and thou givest them
their meat in due season. Thou openest thine hand, and
satisfied the desire of every living thing."

Luke 12:29–31 NIV
"And do not set your heart on what you will eat or drink;
do not worry about it. For the pagan world runs after all
such things, and your Father knows that you need them.
But seek his kingdom, and these things will be given to
you as well."

Chapter 14

Manna in Dry Places

I f you can trust God to walk you through the layoff, you can trust Him to provide all of your needs. He created you, so He has a vested interest in your well being. The Lord is your shepherd through the good times and the desert experience you are in right now.

When we envision a desert, what comes to mind is a vast, dry desolate place where the sun beats down on parched, weary travelers. Surprise! There are life-sustaining resources in the desert, and good shepherds know where to go.

I never understood the responsibility of the shepherd to his sheep until I attended a Bible study where the 23rd Psalm was analyzed in-depth. Sheep only follow the voice of the shepherd, because they have become accustomed to his/her commands to lead them to food and water each day. There are no sprawling green pastures in the desert, but the shepherd knows where to find the sparse grass to feed the sheep.

Sound familiar? When you trust His voice, God will lead you to green pastures to replenish your spirit in a desert experience. Whether you are out of work for a short while or longer than you expected, you will feel God's presence when you stick close by Him.

God won't desert you on the trail as you go through this trial. Are you trusting God to guide you? If not, what's holding you back?

_____

_____

_____

_____

_____

_____

_____

_____

_____

_____

_____

_____

_____

_____

_____

_____

_____

_____

_____

_____

Isaiah 40:31 KJV
"But they that wait upon the Lord shall renew their strength; they shall mount up with wings as eagles; they shall run, and not be weary; and they shall walk, and not faint."

Isaiah 41:10 KJV
"Fear thou not, for I am with thee: be not dismayed; for I am thy God: I will strengthen thee; yea, I will help thee; yea, I will uphold thee with the right hand of my righteousness."

Hebrews 12:2 NIV
"Let us fix our eyes on Jesus, the author and perfecter of our faith, who for the joy set before him endured the cross, scorning its shame, and sat down at the right hand of the throne of God."

Chapter 15

Daily Cup of Still Water

I used to be in such a rush getting ready for work that physical preparation was more of a priority than quiet time with God. I would squeeze in a passage from a meditation booklet while washing my face, brushing my teeth, waiting for the car to warm up in winter, cool down in the summer, or while sitting at a red light. I wasn't focused on what I was reading, it was just part of my daily routine. No matter how relevant the scripture may have been to what was going on in my life, it never had a chance to sink into my spirit.

Since the layoff, I spend quality time with God every day. Throughout the Bible, God tells us how much He loves us and wants us to know Him in a deep, personal relationship. There's no need for a spiritual drought as you walk through the desert.

Quench your thirst each morning with a still cup.

"How do I love thee?" God hasn't bothered to count the ways. He tells us over and over and over in His Word.

SEEDS AND HARVEST

Malachi 3:10–12 KJV
"Bring ye all the tithes into the storehouse, that there may be meat in mine house, and prove me now herewith, saith the Lord of hosts, if I will not open you the windows of heaven, and pour you out a blessing, that there shall not be room enough to receive it."

2 Corinthians 9:6–8 KJV
"But this I say, He who soweth sparingly shall reap also sparingly; and he who soweth bountifully shall reap also bountifully. Every man according as he purposeth in his heart, so let him give; not grudgingly, or of necessity; for God loveth a cheerful giver. And God is able to make all grace abound toward you, that ye, always having all sufficiency in all things, may abound to every good work."

Luke 6:38 NIV
"Give, and it will be given to you. A good measure, pressed down, shaken together and running over, will be poured into your lap. For with the measure you use it will be measured to you."

Chapter 16

God is Still Multiply-ing Fish and Loaves

When you are out of work, the tendency is to count every penny and fret over your income. You have to manage your money wisely, but don't hoard it. If you were already tithing through your church, don't stop. If you have never given at least 10 percent every time you receive income, then now is the time to start.

You probably have less money coming in, but when you give from the heart the amount has no bearing on how God will multiply your offering. Don't try to rationalize that it is better to hold onto the tithe to pay expenses or add to savings. Your faith + seed offering is the best formula for financial stability during this time. God loves to add more when there appears to be less.

In the bible there is a story about Jesus teaching at a large gathering, and at meal time he did not want to send the people away hungry. His disciples did not have enough food to feed the crowd; they only had five small loaves of bread and two fish given by a little boy who was willing to share his lunch. Jesus took the bread and fish and gave thanks to God and instructed his disciples to serve. The disciples were able to feed five thousand, and there were twelve baskets of fragments left over.

God is still creating miracles with our seeds, and He will bless your financial flow when you share every time.

John 15:1–2, 5 NIV
"I am the true vine, and my Father is the gardener. He cuts off every branch in me that bears no fruit, while every branch that does bear fruit he prunes so that it will be even more fruitful."

"I am the vine; you are the branches. If a man remains in me and I in him, he will bear much fruit; apart from me you can do nothing."

1 John 5:4 KJV
"For whatever is born of God overcomes the world. And this is the victory that has overcome the world-our faith."

Psalm 92:12–15 NIV
"The righteous will flourish like a palm tree, they will grow like a cedar of Lebanon, planted in the house of the Lord, they will flourish in the courts of our God . . . They will still bear fruit in old age, they will stay fresh and green, proclaiming, 'The Lord is upright; he is my Rock, and there is no wickedness in him.'"

Chapter 17

Better Not Bitter

When your favorite fruit is in the produce section, but it's not in season, it may not have the familiar good taste. Sometimes our life seems out of sync with the way we think it should go, and we don't feel any joy.

Like the layoff, you may not be happy about it, but it's your season to rest, not work. Could be that God wants to enhance your flavor before the next assignment.

His seeds guarantee fresh produce when the time is ripe.

Psalm 128:1–2 NIV
"Blessed are all who fear the Lord, who walk in his ways. You will eat the fruit of your labor; blessings and prosperity will be yours."

James 1:17–18 NIV
"Every good and perfect gift is from above, coming down from the Father of the heavenly lights, who does not change like shifting shadows. He chose to give us birth through the word of truth, that we might be a kind of firstfruits of all he created."

James 3:17 NIV
"But the wisdom that comes from heaven is first of all pure; then peace-loving, considerate, submissive, full of mercy and good fruit, impartial and sincere."

Chapter 18

* *

Strange Fruit

How many times has God planted a seed in us to try something that we have never done before? We neglected to water the thought because we couldn't move beyond our comfort zone. The intended harvest never comes to fruition because we didn't see ourselves in that particular role.

We all have a special job to do while we are here. Your next position could be a direct link to God's purpose for your life. The layoff is the seed that planted you in fertile ground to cultivate exciting growth in your life.

Rest assured, you will be successful, because God's harvest is top quality, even if it's strange fruit.

Proverbs 22:1 NIV
"A good name is more desirable than great riches; to be esteemed is better than silver or gold."

Proverbs 22:4 NIV
"Humility and the fear of the Lord bring wealth and honor and life."

Proverbs 23:4–5 NIV
"Do not wear yourself out to get rich; have the wisdom to show restraint. Cast but a glance at riches, and they are gone, for they will surely sprout wings and fly off to the sky like an eagle."

Ecclesiastes 7:11–12 NIV
"Wisdom, like an inheritance, is a good thing and benefits those who see the sun. Wisdom is a shelter as money is a shelter, but the advantage of knowledge is this: that wisdom preserves the life of its possessor."

Chapter 19

Trust Fund

W hether you are male, female, single, married, young, or a senior citizen, employed or unemployed, you don't have to be a millionaire to benefit from a trust fund.

Try this: Take out a penny, a nickel, a dime, a quarter, and now a dollar. When you look them over you will see a familiar phrase on each piece of currency, "In God We Trust." Do just that.

Keep your hands open to receive as well as give.

NETWORKING

Psalm 16:5–6 NIV
"Lord, you have assigned me my portion and my cup; you have made my lot secure. The boundary lines have fallen for me in pleasant places; surely I have a delightful inheritance."

2 Corinthians 4:8–9 KJV
"We are troubled on every side, yet not distressed; we are perplexed, but not in despair; persecuted, but not forsaken; cast down, but not destroyed."

Roman 12:12 KJV
"Rejoicing in hope; patient in tribulation; continuing constant in prayer."

Chapter 20

Tell Them as a Testimony

You must tell others that you are in the job market, because you never know who God is going to use to make the right connection for you. The key is not to whine. Let everyone know you are trusting God for your next position.

You don't need anyone's pity, and contacts will be much more receptive to passing on your resume when you have a positive attitude. Be a walking testimony that your faith will pay off.

You will be an inspiration to those who are watching you. They may have to travel the same road one day.

2 Corinthians 1:3–4 KJV
"Blessed be God, even the Father of our Lord Jesus Christ, the Father of mercies, and the God of all comfort, Who comforteth us in all our tribulation, that we may be able to comfort them who are in any trouble, by the comfort with which we ourselves are comforted of God."

Romans 12:15 KJV
"Rejoice with them that do rejoice, and weep with them that weep."

2 Peter 1:5–8 NIV
"For this very reason, make every effort to add to your faith goodness; and to goodness, knowledge, and to knowledge, self-control; and to self-control, perseverance; and to perseverance, godliness, and to godliness, brotherly kindness, and to brotherly kindness, love. For if you possess these qualities in increasing measure, they will keep you from being ineffective and unproductive in your knowledge of our Lord Jesus Christ."

Chapter 21
You're Much Stronger Than a Cupcake

It's important not to turn away from others during this time. Don't hibernate. Share your faith with others who have been downsized. Remind them that their talents and skills will be utilized again. Someone needs to hear from you so they won't feel wounded and alone. It's okay for you seek encouragement, too!

There was a box of green cupcakes in my refrigerator. Originally there were nine in three rows of three. One cupcake was left in the first row, and the remaining two rows were full. The lone cupcake kept tipping over even though I repeatedly propped it against the nearest row. After each fall, the frosting smeared more and more and it began to crumble. I felt sorry for it, so I ate it.

Don't crumble. Lean on a close network of family and friends who are there for you.

Matthew 6:27 NIV
"Who of you by worrying can add a single hour to his life?"

Psalm 31:7–8 KJV
"I will be glad and rejoice in thy mercy; for thou hast considered my trouble; thou hast known my soul in adversities, And hast not shut me up into the hand of the enemy. Thou hast set my feet in a large room."

Isaiah 43:2 KJV
"When thou passest through the waters, I will be with thee; and through the rivers, they shall not overflow thee; When thou walkest through the fire, thou shalt not be burned, neither shall the flame kindle upon thee."

Chapter 22

Avoid the Infamous Trio

Be careful. Some people can get stuck on "Why did this happen to me?" Maybe you asked the same question, but you have moved on without bitterness over the layoff. Others may not share your optimism and refuse to leave their self-imposed pity party. Encourage them and be supportive. If they want to stay in that mode, keep moving.

It may seem cruel, but it's not. You can pray for them without keeping company. Don't adapt to their attitude.

If you can't associate with anybody but God, it's okay because He's there for you. He understands why you are smiling. You are tied in to the right network, and there is no reason to hang out with the three amigos: worry, doubt, and fear.

NEXT!

Psalm 16:5–6 NIV
"Lord, you have assigned me my portion and my cup; you have made my lot secure. The boundary lines have fallen for me in pleasant places; surely I have a delightful inheritance."

2 Corinthians 9:8 KJV
"And God is able to make all grace abound toward you; that ye, always having sufficiency in all (things), may abound to every good work."

Proverbs 12:14 NIV
"From the fruit of his lips a man is filled with good things as surely as the work of his hands rewards him."

Chapter 23
You Will Work Again

It may be a while, but the next job will come in due time. It is your responsibility to look for a job, but you don't have to do it eight hours a day. That can be stressful, and you need balance to stay positive and motivated.

Whenever you send out a resume or make a cold call, pray. Your prayer can be as simple as "Lord if this is the right job for me, thank You. If not, I will wait for the one You are sending." If you take this approach, you will have peace when you don't land an interview for what appeared to be the ideal job.

As you read the "Thanks, but no thanks" replies, remember you were not selected because God has to keep you available for the position He has already chosen.

Don't take in all the negative statistics and data on rising unemployment and the slow economy. All you need is *one* job, and God has put your name on it. He will let you know when it's time to start.

If the months of unemployment stretch on and you are almost down to your last dollar, do you believe that God will provide the right job when you need it?

_____

_____

_____

_____

_____

_____

_____

_____

_____

_____

_____

_____

_____

_____

_____

_____

_____

_____

Psalm 143:1 NIV
"O Lord, hear my prayer, listen to my cry for mercy; in your faithfulness and righteousness come to my relief."

Isaiah 50:4
"The Sovereign Lord has given me an instructed tongue, to know the word that sustains the weary. He wakens me morning by morning, wakens my ear to listen like one being taught."

Isaiah 65:24
"Before they call I will answer; while they are still speaking I will hear."

Chapter 24

A Comes Before B, but Follows G

You are going to strategize and make daily to-do lists to orchestrate your job search. It's what you are supposed to do. You feel proactive and sort of in control. Whether you fill up your days networking, searching through the paper, or on the internet, it will become frustrating when nothing turns up around the six-month mark. Low self-esteem might creep up and money worries, too.

You will move into your ABC mode of operation. You visualize plan A. If that doesn't work, you move to plan B. No results, then on to plan C. When all else fails, there's plan G. Plan G is God.

While we have been strategizing and stressing, God has already worked out the ABCs of the layoff. He's lined up the next Assignment, Benefits, and Compensation package.

You won't be worried if you begin with G before planning ABC. It's divine order.

Surrendering to God's will is not deflating; it will empower you. What plans will you turn over to Him?

_____

_____

_____

_____

_____

_____

_____

_____

_____

_____

_____

_____

_____

_____

_____

_____

_____

_____

_____

_____

Ephesians 2:10 NIV
"For we are God's workmanship, created in Christ Jesus to do good works, which God prepared in advance for us to do."

Romans 8:28 KJV
"And we know that all things work together for good to them that love God, to them who are the called according to his purpose."

1 Peter 5:6 NIV
"Humble yourselves, therefore, under God's mighty hand, that he may lift you up in due time. Cast all your anxiety on him because he cares for you."

Chapter 25

A Labor Pain is Nothing to God

A female carries a baby for approximately nine months. Sometimes God has to carry our purpose for decades before He delivers it into our spirit.

Now that you have some free time, God can get your attention. Be quiet and listen. He can tell you the purpose He has been holding in safekeeping until now.

New beginnings are often birthed after pain has subsided. The job loss was the entry to your new beginning; walk through it with faith. It won't be long before you will understand why it had to be this way. Then you can celebrate.

When God created heaven and earth, He also had you in mind. There's always been a higher purpose for your existence over and above your regular job.

Do you know why you're here?

_____

_____

_____

_____

_____

_____

_____

_____

_____

_____

_____

_____

_____

_____

_____

_____

_____

_____

Habakkuk 2:3 KJV
"For the vision is yet for an appointed time, but at the
end it shall speak, and not lie; though it tarry, wait for it,
because it will surely come, it will not tarry."

Ephesians 1:11–12 NIV
"In him we were also chosen, having been predestined
according to the plan of him who works out everything
in conformity with the purpose of his will, in order that
we, who were the first to hope in Christ, might be for
the praise of his glory."

2 Timothy 1:7 NIV
"For God did not give us a spirit of timidity, but a spirit
of power, of love and of self-discipline."

Chapter 26

. . . . .

You Too Can
Be a Sheep Dog

In the movie "Babe," the talking-animal story revolved around a pig on the farm who was kind, humble and had a giving spirit. Babe wasn't content just to hang around a trough or roll in the mud. He admired the way the two sheep dogs helped the farmer with the flock. Babe had the desire and eagerness to become a sheep dog, too.

Through a turn of events, he finally got his chance to help with the sheep. The other animals laughed at him, but Babe persevered and won the farmer's trust. At the end of the movie, Babe and the farmer stood side by side after winning a major competition as both their dreams came true.

It's like your daydreams. The same dream that would creep up when you were working. You pictured something completely different than your day job, maybe the hobby you love to do in your spare time. In the dream you were successful because you were happy.

Your dreams may have a huge impact on your next source of income. Even if you had to make less money, would it be worth it to go for your big blue ribbon? Do you have faith in God to step out into a different role despite what others think you should be doing?

Go ahead, be brave. Be a sheep dog.

Proverbs 3:5–6 KJV
"Trust in the Lord with all thine heart; and lean not unto thine own understanding. In all thy ways acknowledge him, and he shall direct thy paths."

Psalm 32:8 NIV
"I will instruct you and teach you in the way you should go; I will counsel you and watch over you."

2 Corinthians 12:9 NIV
"My grace is sufficient for you, for my power is made perfect in weakness."

Chapter 27

* *

Easing Toward
the White Flower

One morning before Sunday school, a good friend gave me an inspirational birthday card. After reading it, I blurted, "Now I'm really afraid. I guess I will have to do what God is telling me to do." Without asking what, the teacher said, "If you have faith, you aren't supposed to be afraid." She closed the lesson book and asked me if I would help demonstrate how to walk by faith.

I was blindfolded with a scarf, and the room was turned into an obstacle course. I followed my teacher's voice around twists and turns to reach a prize on the other side of the room. The class also called out instructions. I was uncomfortable because I wasn't in control, but they kept reassuring me they wouldn't let anything happen to me along the way. When I reached the other side, my blindfold was removed. I opened my eyes and faced a beautiful white flower arrangement. The walk was worth it; I hadn't noticed it before. Sometimes others can see what's on the other side before we do. God may choose someone close or even a stranger to help us reach our goal.

Shortly after my layoff, a friend phoned and asked, "What are you doing? I pictured you walking your dog then sitting down with a big cup of tea to write at the computer." She was right on target, but scrap the tea and computer. I prefer a warm mug of cranberry juice and pencil and paper.

Glad she couldn't see my warm cotton footies with holes.

EPILOGUE

Hebrews 6:17–19 NIV
"Because God wanted to make the unchanging nature of his purpose very clear to the heirs of what was promised, he confirmed it with an oath. God did this so that, by two unchangeable things in which it is impossible for God to lie, we who have fled to take hold of the hope offered to us may be greatly encouraged. We have this hope as an anchor for the soul, firm and secure."

1 Peter 4:19 NIV
"So then, those who suffer according to God's will should commit themselves to their faithful Creator and continue to do good."

John 3:16 NIV *16:33*
"I have told you these things, so that in me you may have peace. In this world you will have trouble. But take heart! I have overcome the world."

Downsized Up
Nightstands Don't Have to Be Classy

W hen you look at the bedroom decor in magazines, the nightstands sometimes showcase antique lamps, expensive picture frames, and crystal vases with fresh-cut flowers. It's beautiful, but not practical for me.

My night table holds a discount-store lamp, alarm clock, notepads, and a plastic pencil holder filled with pens and paper clips. My table is not pretty, but it's practical, having the items I need within easy reach.

My layoff experience did not fall into a common scenario—lose job, become consumed with job search, beat yourself up over length of job search, and tell yourself it's practical to end job search by accepting a job you don't really want.

We are always told by ones in the spiritual know to look at God and not at the circumstances. If you can tell yourself every day that God will send you the right job under the right circumstances at the right time, then you can search with hope and anticipation. That did it for me. It brought me into a comfort zone I have never experienced before. I trusted God for the next step whenever doubt tried to take over. My job was to stay connected and wait.

Your experience does not have to fall into a certain pattern that looks or feels like anyone else's. You could end up better off than you were before the downsizing, happier and more prosperous. You can also emerge with deeper spiritual grounding and stronger faith as an added bonus.

That's beautiful and practical.

TEN THINGS TO CONSIDER WHILE YOU ARE IN TRANSITION

1.

Tell Your Children The Truth

If your children are old enough to understand, tell them that you won't be working for a while. They need to know the truth, because it will affect the family. You may have to cut down on some activities to watch expenses, and they may even be helpful in those decisions.

They will appreciate having you around more. Now you can also make those late-afternoon teachers conferences and sporting events.

2.

Don't Stress Out Your Kids

Latchkey kids may begin to feel like you have invaded their space. Let them enjoy downtime after they come home from school. Remember, they have been on their own while you finished out the work day. Don't start in right away with homework and chores as soon as they hit the door.

3.

What Should I Tell My Neighbors?

Don't be ashamed and pretend you are working from home or taking a sabbatical. Be honest. You are supposed to tell everyone you know that you are unemployed because you never know where the next job lead will come from.

Besides, if they haven't gone through the same experience, most likely they know someone who has.

4.

IF YOU ARE HAVING A BAD DAY, HAVE IT!

If you need to blow off your job search for an entire day, do it without guilt. Take care of some personal projects, hang out with some friends (who may also be unemployed), or don't do anything.

The want ads, internet, and employment agencies will still be there the next day, and you can take up where you left off with a new attitude.

5.

THERE'S MORE THAN ONE WAY TO BRING HOME THE BACON

Sign up with a temporary agency. Or, if possible, market yourself as an independent consultant in your field. You will be generating income while you search for a full-time position and make some great contacts in the process.

6.

MAINTAIN YOUR FRIENDSHIPS AT THE COMPANY

If they are true friends, you should have no resentment because they are still working and you are no longer there.

They will need your support, because it will probably be a bumpy ride for those left behind after a layoff.

7.

TAKE TIME OUT TO LEND A HAND

Your hours of service are no longer defined between 8:00am–5:00pm, but someone, somewhere needs you everyday.

This goes beyond your immediate family. Help out in your community. Your kindness will be rewarded.

8.

LET THEM DO THEIR JOB

Don't call your relatives and friends during office hours and tie them up with long conversations. They have work to do, and so do you!

9.

STAGNANT WATER NEVER SMELLS SWEET

It's okay to reminisce about the good old days, but don't get stuck there. You have too much to do in the present, and even more to accomplish in the future.

10.

TAKE GOOD CARE OF YOURSELF

A healthy spirit, mind, and body is the best passport for all of the wonderful adventures ahead of you.

Isaiah 43:18–19 NIV
"Forget the former things; do not dwell on the past. See,
I am doing a new thing! Now it springs up; do you not
perceive it?"

To order additional copies of

Downsized UP

Have your credit card ready and call:

1-877-421-READ (7323)

or please visit our web site at
www.pleasantword.com

Also available at:
www.amazon.com
www.BarnesandNoble.com
www.Christianbooks.com